FORWARD

The information contained in this book has been distilled from many years of teaching experience. It is our intention to pass on this information as it has been successfully used with positive results for many years. Teaching professionals differ in their approach as to what works for them in their practices. Years of professional experience have taught us to encourage each individual student to do what works for him or her, to get the most positive results in the shortest length of time. The goal of this book is to cover the basics of learning drums from a popular music standpoint, not from a schooled, disciplined approach. The idea is to have fun with the instrument. We certainly encourage private instruction whenever possible. Any knowledge gained in the pursuit of learning the instrument can only be helpful. *-Dave Beyer and Larry Little*

INTRODUCTION

Larry Little's "Learn Drums Book" volume 1 can be used as a stand alone learning, practice, and study guide, or with the video "Learn Drums on VCR" volume 1. The numbers on the bottom corners of each page provide a reference guide to help you coordinate the use of the book with the video tape. By using the fast forward or reverse on your tape machine you can locate and review sections of the video tape that correspond with the book. You can also use the digital counter found on most VCR machines. To do this, reset your VCR counter at the beginning of the tape where the video clock first appears. Then as you play through the tape, take note of the different sections you want to review by writing down the counter numbers in the blank space provided next to the video clock numbers listed in the book.

The exercise drum charts correspond with the songs found in the "video songbook" section of Larry Little's "Learn Drums on VCR" volume 1 video. This book is written from a right-handed point of view. For those of you who are left-handed, it is recommended to set up the drum kit as pictured <u>and</u> reversed to discover which is best for you. Now let's "LEARN DRUMS".

TABLE OF CONTENTS

LARRY  LITTLE'S

LEARN DRUMS BOOK

VOLUME 1

BY DAVE BEYER & LARRY LITTLE

Editors: Mathew Dalessi, SLG, Inc., and Larry Little
Graphic Design: CDS Graphics, Glendale, CA and Larry Little
Photography: Phi Vu

BY DAVE BEYER & LARRY LITTLE

Printed in USA

ISBN 1-884208-09-6

THE LARRY LITTLE COMPANY
P. O. BOX 413005 SUITE#101
NAPLES, FLORIDA 33941-3005

GENERAL DRUM INFORMATION

Drum Parts

The standard drum set is made up of 9 pieces.

The Snare Drum

The Bass Drum

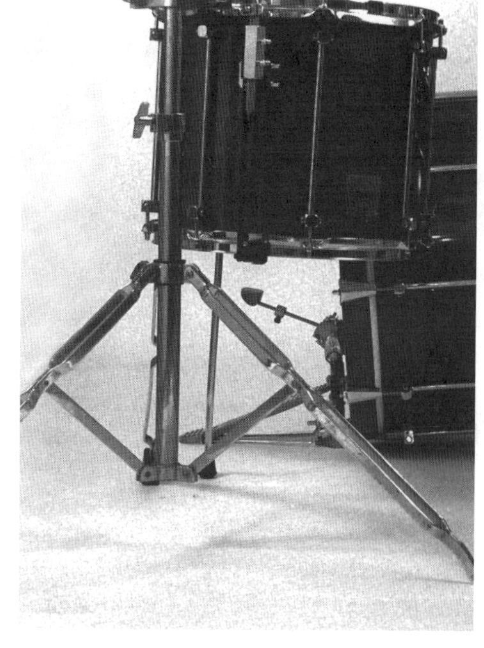

3 Toms

(Two toms can either be mounted on top of the bass drum or on stands while the floor tom sits on the floor).

The Ride Cymbal

2 Crash Cymbals

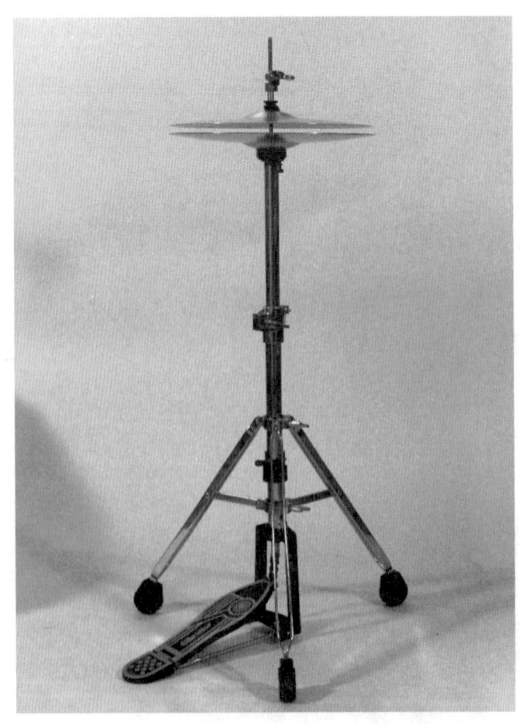

A Pair of Hi-Hat Cymbals

Setting Up The Drums

The arrangement and the setup of the drum set is simple. First set up the bass drum, adjusting the legs or the "spurs" of the bass drum so the front bottom is about two inches off the ground.

Next, attach the foot pedal to the back hoop of the bass drum.

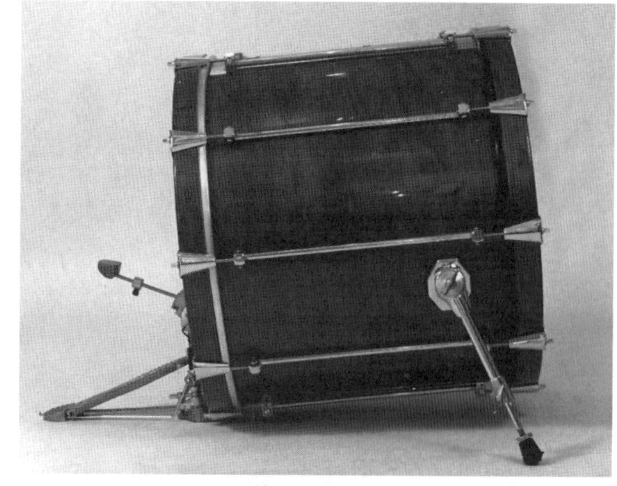

Attach the tom-toms to either the tom-tom mounts on the bass drum or to the stands, depending on your set-up. Make sure they are in a comfortable playing position–not too high, not too low.

Tom-tom mounts

Tom-toms

Position the floor tom to the right side of the bass drum. Adjust one leg so the drum is tilted toward you.

Snare throw-off

Next, set up the snare drum. Make sure the "snare throw-off" is in a comfortable place so you can get to it easily.

Angle the snare drum slightly toward you.

When the drums are put together to make a set, they should look like this:

Front View

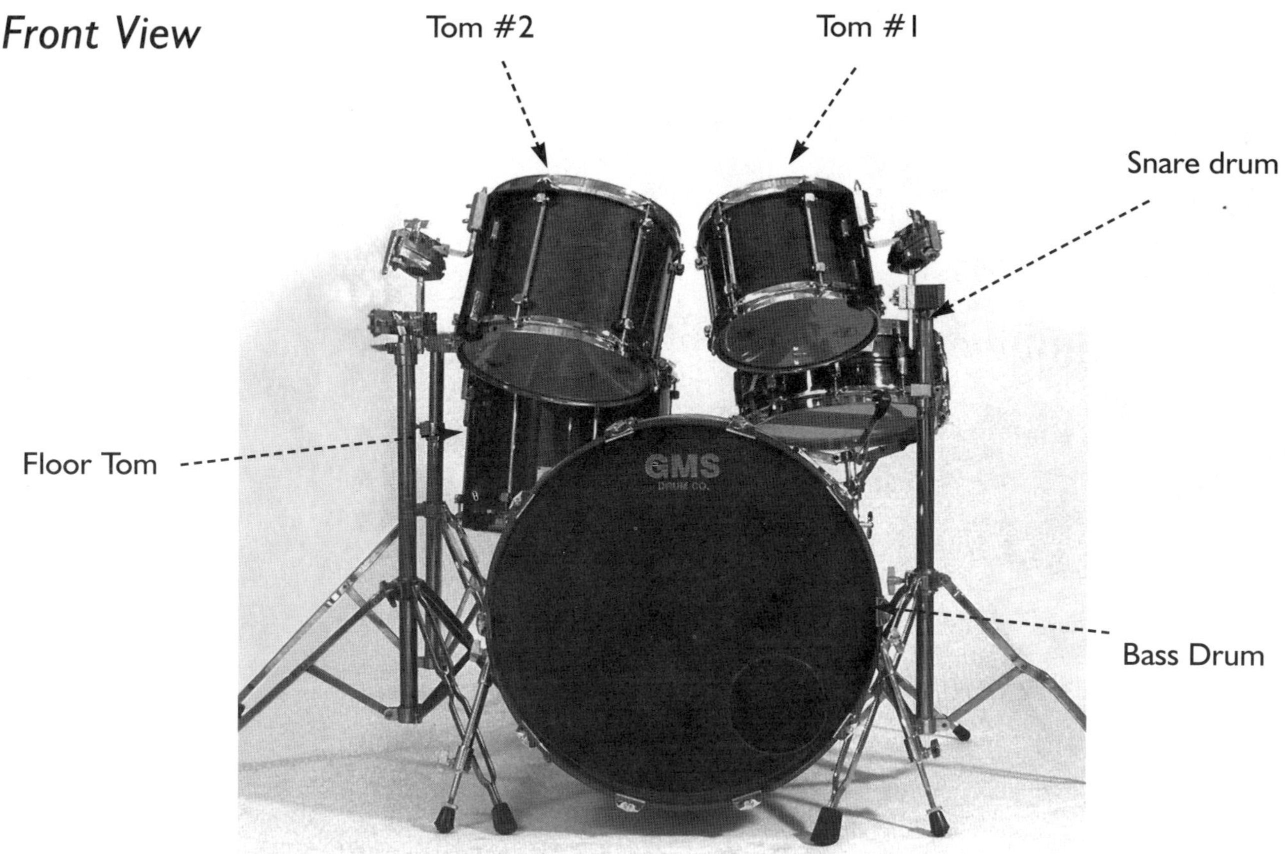

Rear View

This completes the drum part of a drum set, but no set is complete without cymbals.

Setting Up The Cymbals

Tom #2

Ride Cymbal

The ride cymbal is slightly larger and thicker than the crash cymbals. The ride is usually placed to the right side, just above the second tom.

Tom #1

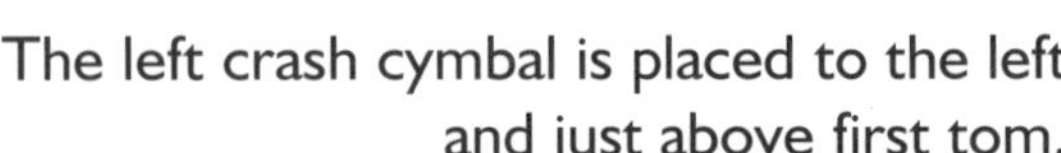

The left crash cymbal is placed to the left and just above first tom.

Right Crash Cymbal

The right crash cymbal is placed to the right of the ride cymbal and above the floor tom.

To set up the hi-hat, first put the bottom cymbal on the hi-hat stand.

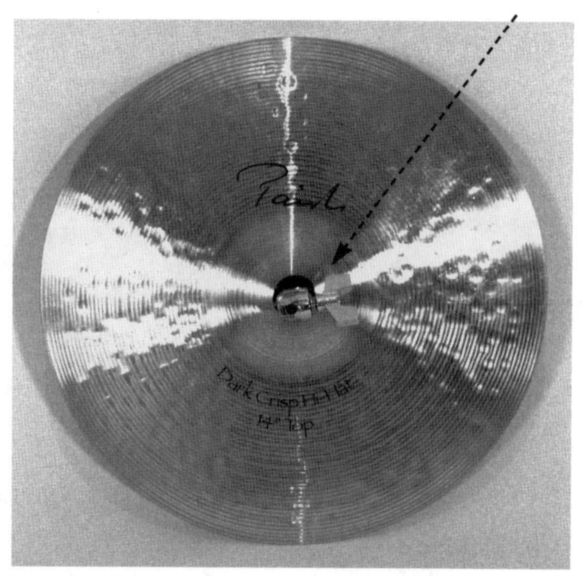

Place the hi-hat clutch on the top cymbal.

Slide the top cymbal onto the rod of the hi-hat stand. Push the pedal down (about one inch or so); then tighten the wing nut on the clutch.

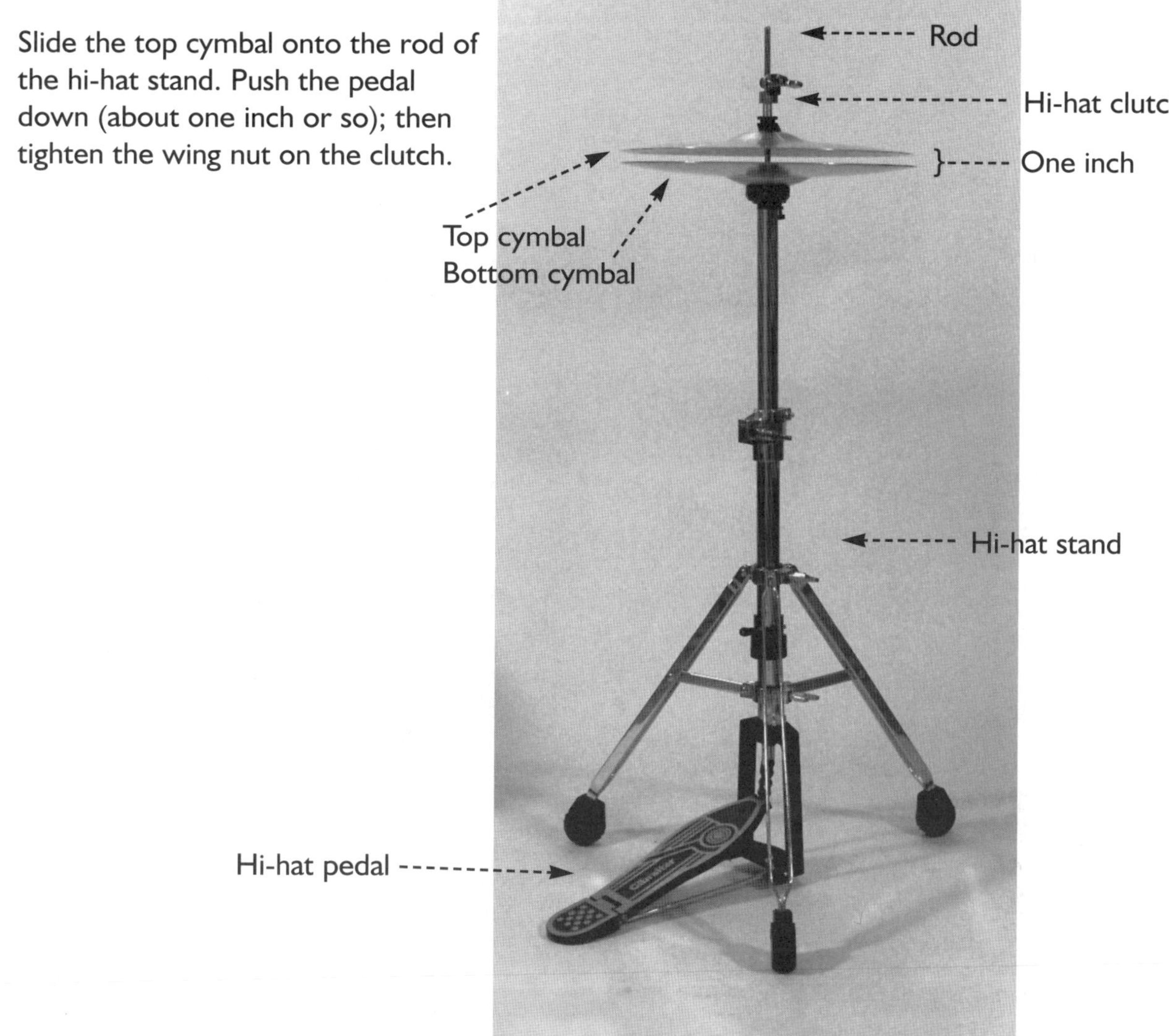

GENERAL DRUM INFORMATION

When the drum set is completely set up and ready to play, it should look something like this:

Front View

Rear View

**Note: This is a basic 9-piece drum set. Some drummers use more pieces; some use less.*

Drum Accessories

There are many accessories you can add to your drum set. One of the most useful is a "stick bag", to carry your sticks, brushes, and tools.

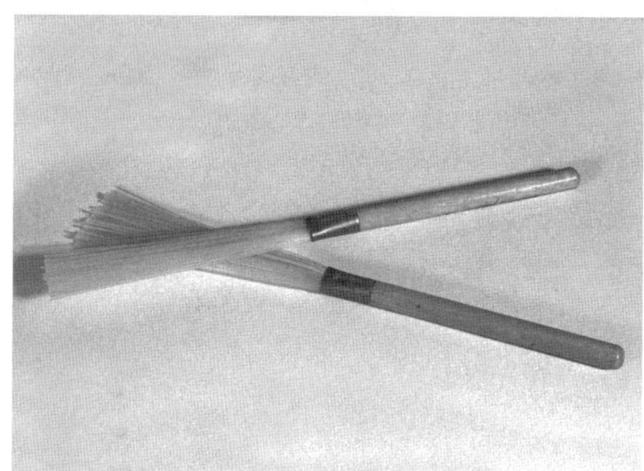

Brushes

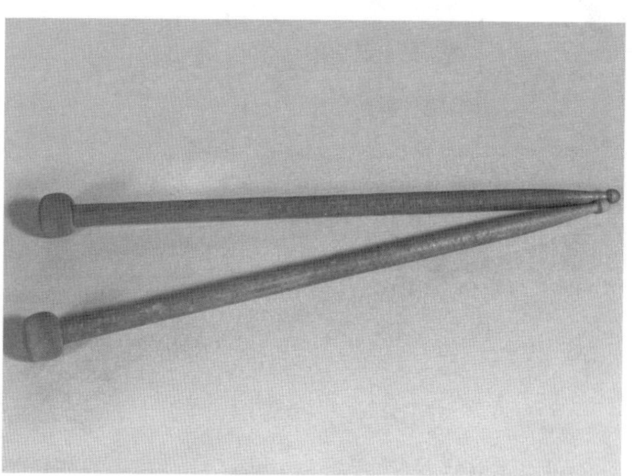

Mallets

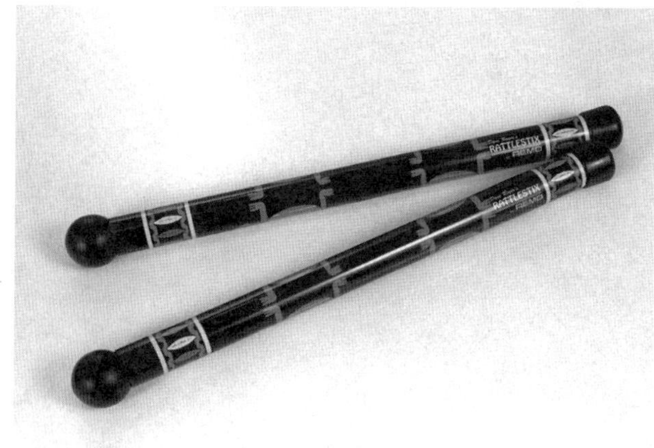

Rattlestix

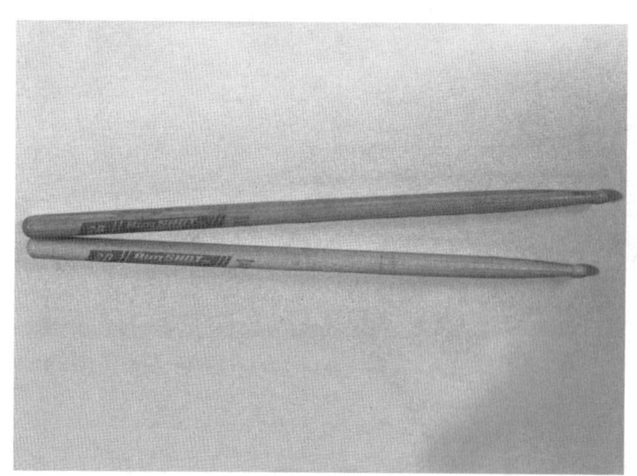

Conventional wooden drumsticks

DRUM TUNING

Take your drumsticks and hit the snare drum, toms, and the bass drum. Notice how they sound. They may not be in tune. Drums can go in and out of tune. The first time you put together your set, you'll need to tune the drums. From time to time after that you'll also need to make minor tuning adjustments.

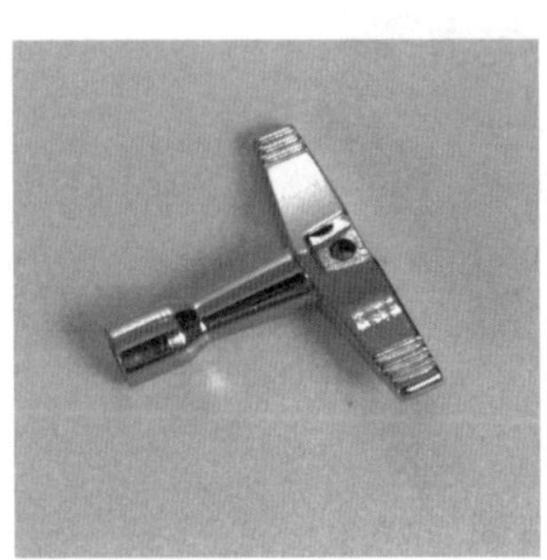

Drum key

Snare throw-off

Take a drumstick in one hand and a drum key in the other. Turn the snares off by pulling down the snare throw-off.

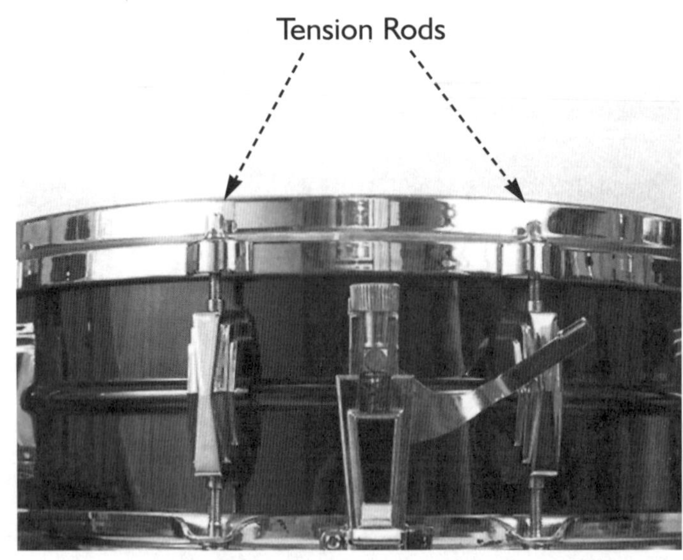

Tension Rods

Tension Rods

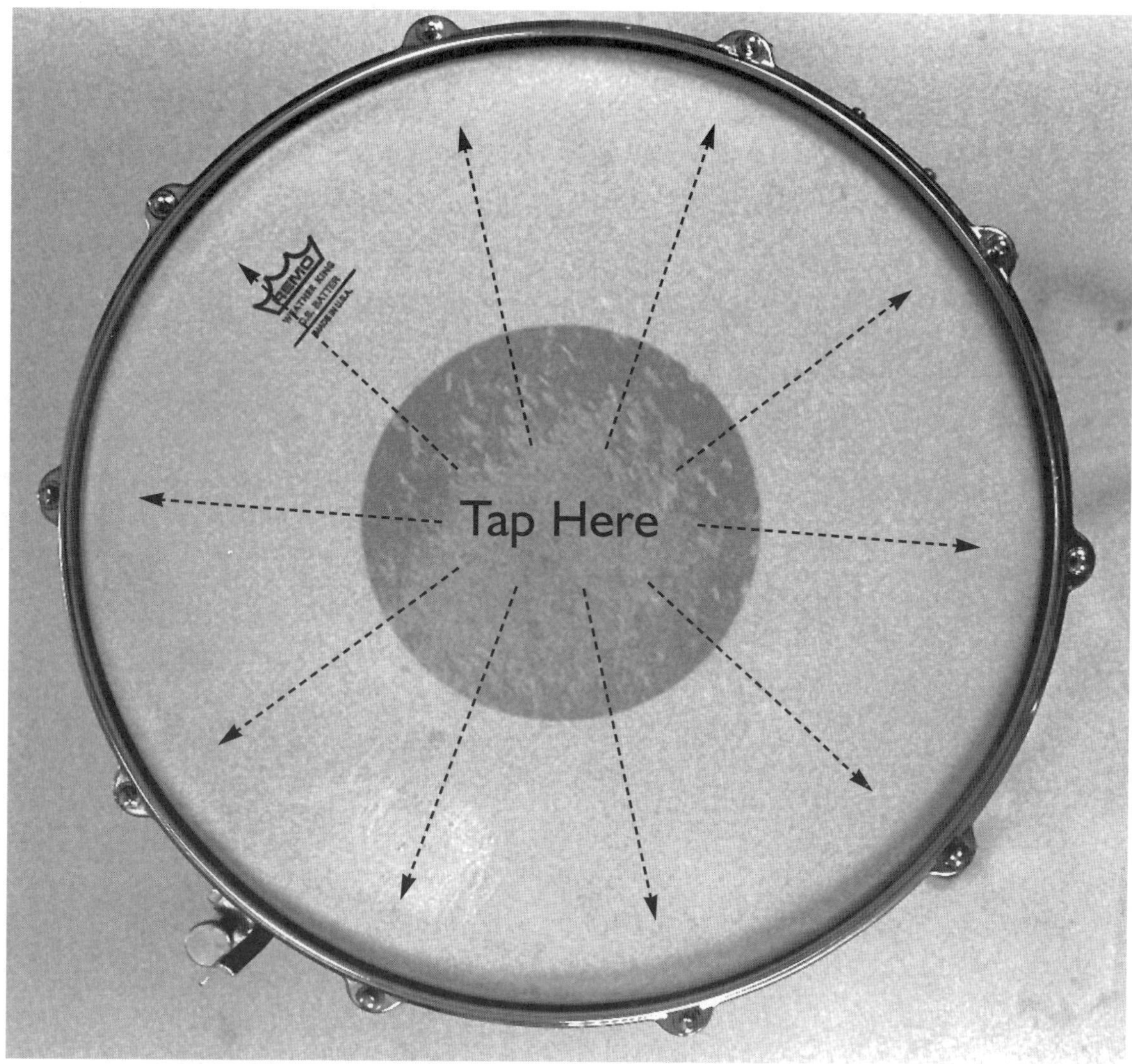

Start by tapping the drumhead about one inch from the rim of the snare drum in front of each tension rod.

Tip: Make sure to tap in front of each tension rod.

In certain areas you might notice a different sound (called a pitch). It might sound high in some places and low in other places. The idea is to get the drumhead to sound the same all the way around. How high or how low the pitch is, is up to you. In general, the snare drum is tuned higher than the other drums. Using the drum key, tighten or loosen the tension rods. When your drum is in tune, every place you hit should sound the same. Use the same procedure to tune the rest of your drums.

**Note: The bottom head should be tuned to the same pitch as the top head.*

TUNING TIPS:

- The 1st tom should be tuned a little lower in pitch than the snare drum.
- The 2nd tom should be tuned a little lower in pitch than the 1st tom.
- The floor tom should be tuned a little lower in pitch than the 2nd tom.
- The bass drum is tuned the lowest.

**Note: For most styles of playing, drummers like a muffled bass drum sound. To get this sound, place a small pillow or blanket inside the drum. The purpose of this is to deaden the sound of the bass drum. Also, some drummers use duct tape on the drum heads to get rid of any unwanted ring.*

**Note: Tuning a drum takes practice and patience, so don't get frustrated on your first try. You will soon develop an ear for tuning and you can still play the drums even if they aren't perfectly in tune.*

PLAYING TECHNIQUE

Drumsticks come in different thicknesses for different styles of music. To get started, you can use any type. There are two standard ways of holding the drumsticks:

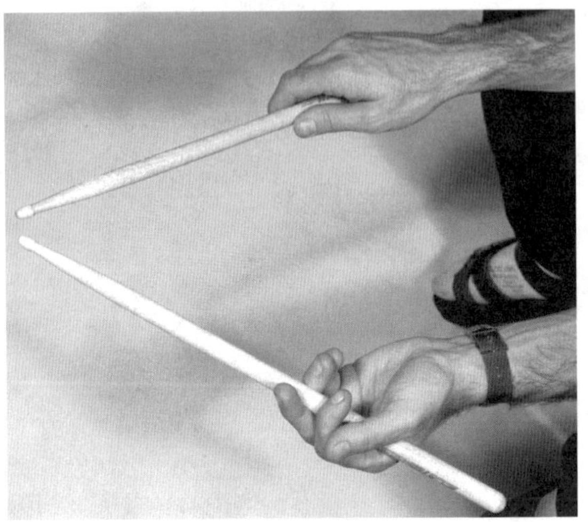

The traditional style

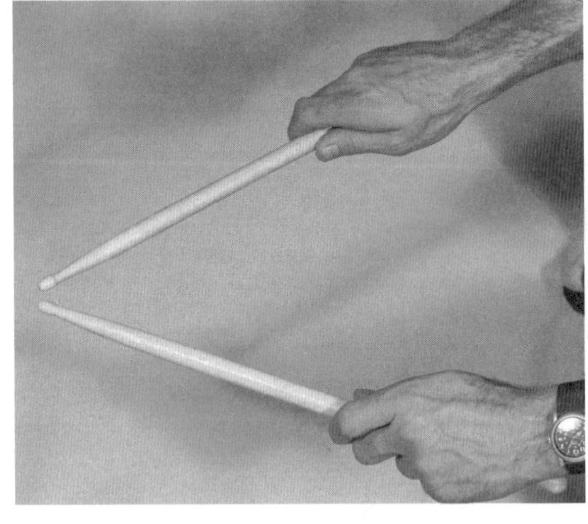

The match grip style

For the purpose of this book, use the match grip style.

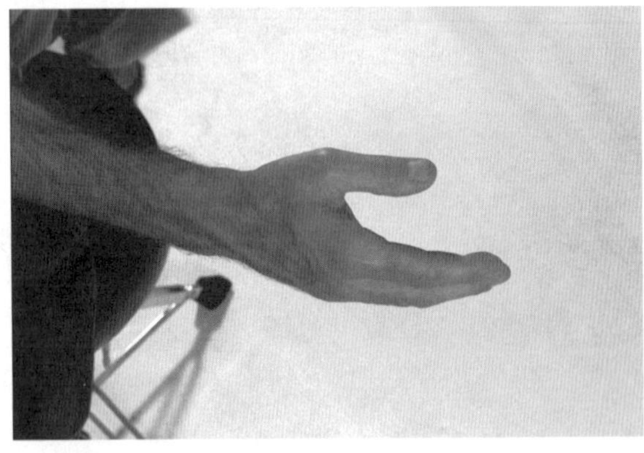

Hold out your right hand like you're going to shake hands.

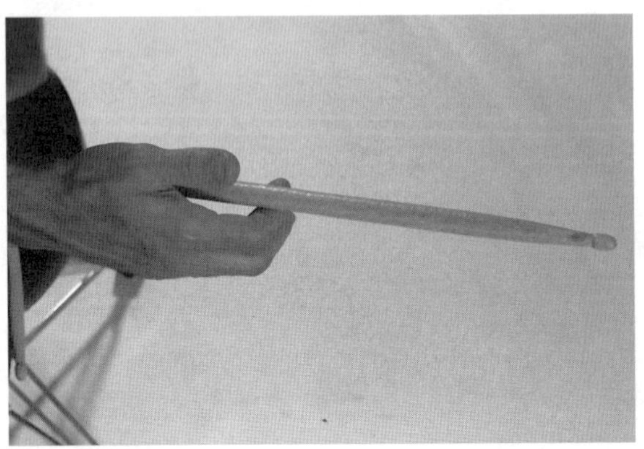

Bend your index finger and place the stick against your first knuckle.

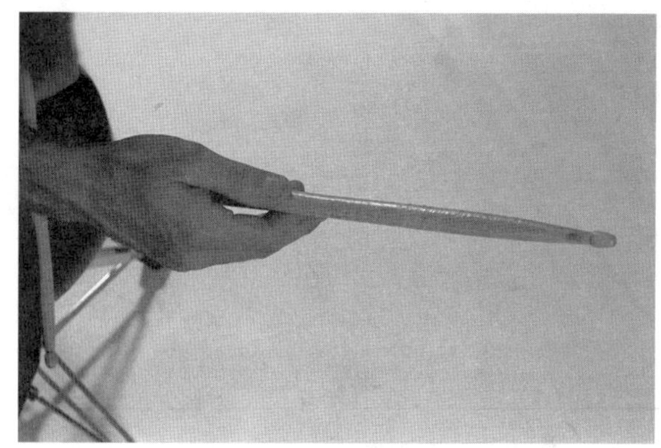

Put your right thumb directly on top of the stick.

Wrap your other 3 fingers around the stick without squeezing too hard.

Do the same with your left hand.

**Note: Most of the pressure is between your index finger and your thumb.*

Hold both sticks (with your thumbs on top) out in front of you.

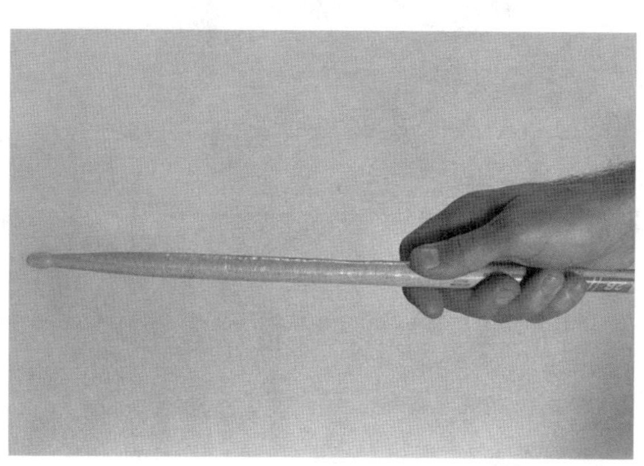

Now your right hand is in the perfect position to play the ride cymbal.

When you play the drums, turn the tops of your hands over slightly, so they are almost flat.

This allows you to use a combination of a wrist stroke and a finger stroke. Use these two types of strokes together. **Note: The wrist bends slightly and the fingers help move the stick.*

Wrist Stroke

Finger Stroke

Stroke Exercise #1

The first exercise will involve just the snare drum. Play four strokes with each hand. Count as you play each stroke. Repeat this exercise until it sounds even and smooth.

R=right hand
L=left hand

count: 1 2 3 4 1 2 3 4 1 2 3 4 1 2 3 4
play: R R R R L L L L R R R R L L L L

Tip: Make sure you are keeping an even pace as you play. You might want to purchase a metronome to play along with and help you keep a steady beat.

Stroke Exercise #2 (Alternating Strokes)

The second exercise is the same as the first exercise except this time use alternating strokes.

R=right hand
L=left hand

count: 1 2 3 4 1 2 3 4 1 2 3 4 1 2 3 4
play: R L R L R L R L R L R L R L R L

Making Up Your Own Stroke Exercises

A good way to practice is to make up your own combination of strokes. Here are some examples of different stroke combinations:

Stroke Combination Example #1

(always count as you play)
count: 1 2 3 4 1 2 3 4 1 2 3 4 1 2 3 4
play: R R L L R R L L R R L L R R L L

slow to fast + fast to slow

Stroke Combination Example #2

count: 1 2 3 4 1 2 3 4 1 2 3 4 1 2 3 4
play: R L R R L R L L R L R R L R L L

Paradiddle

Following these examples, use the space provided on page 38 to write your own stroke combinations.

Foot Technique

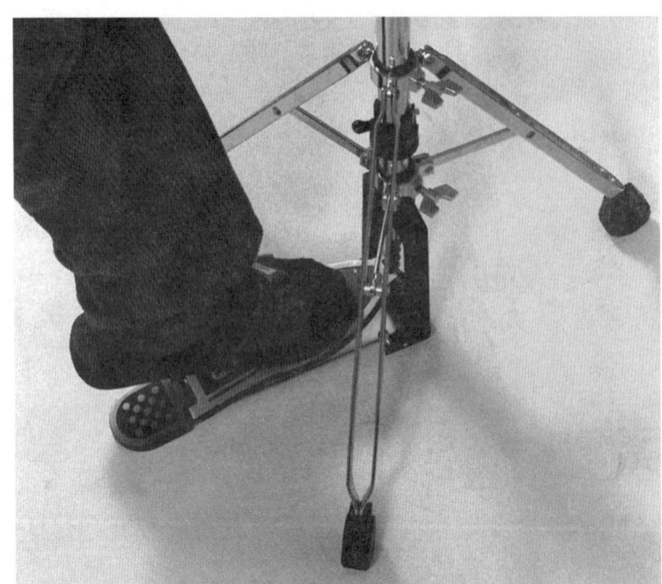

When you play the bass drum and hi-hat, you usually keep your heels up and play with your toes.

Foot Exercise

Try these alternating strokes with the foot pedals.

Left foot> hi-hat
Right foot> bass drum

count: 1 2 3 4 1 2 3 4 1 2 3 4 1 2 3 4
play: R L R L R L R L R L R L R L R L
(with feet)

**Note: Using your feet, practice the same stroke combinations you did with your hands.*

COMPOSING DRUMBEATS

**Note: You can learn to compose and play drumbeats by listening to and imitating the drums you hear on Larry Little's "Learn Drums on VCR" volume 1 and by following the patterns starting on page 24.*

Standard Drum Musical Notation

A "staff" of lines and spaces is used to write out different combinations of strokes and beats on the drums. This is called "standard drum musical notation".

The Staff

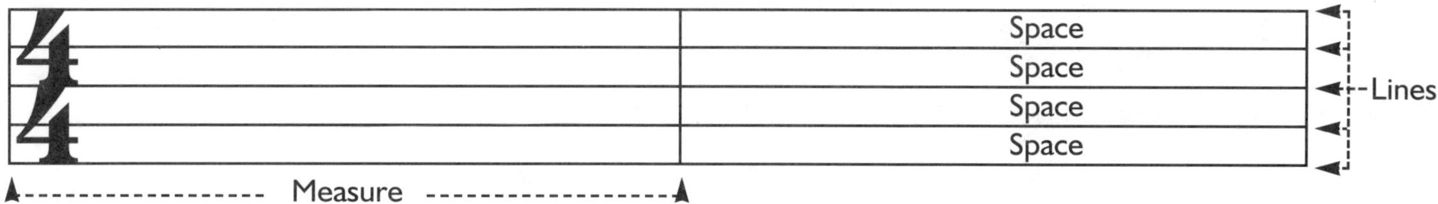

**Note: A measure or a bar is one section of musical time.*

4/4 time means 4 beats to a measure; a quarter note gets one beat.

Quarter note:

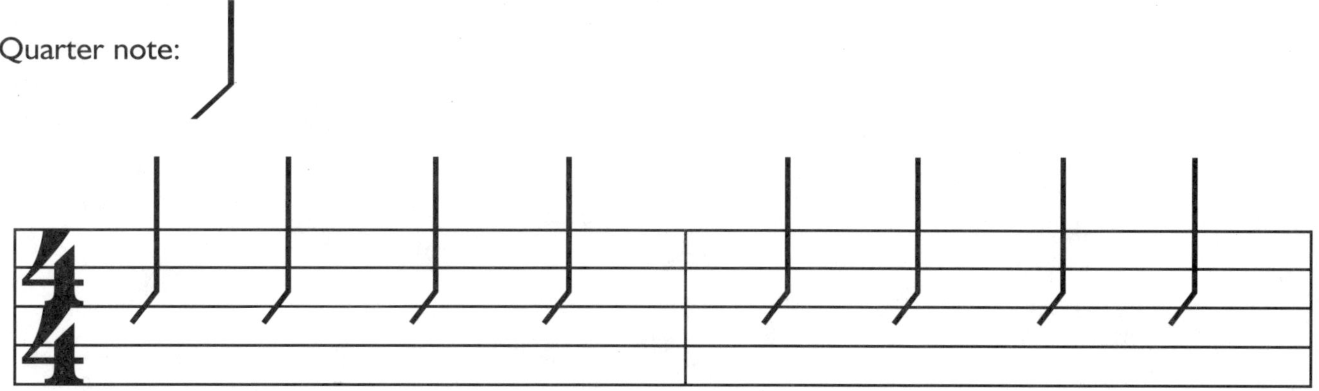

Musical time can be divided into quarters. In this case, there are four quarter notes in each measure.

Cymbal/Hi-Hat

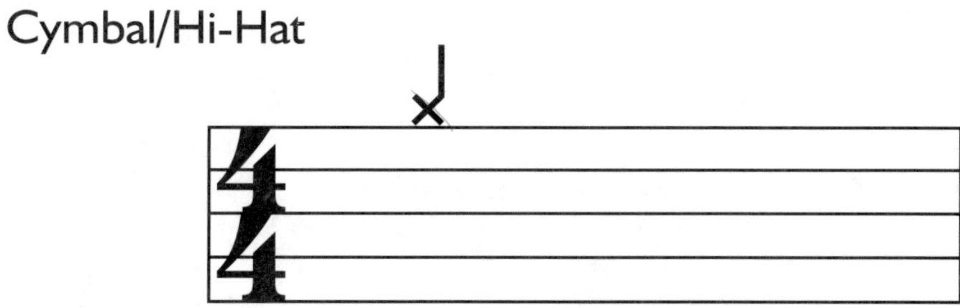

Notes are placed on the staff to tell you which drum or cymbal to play. All hi-hat and cymbal parts are written as an "x" and sit on top of the staff.

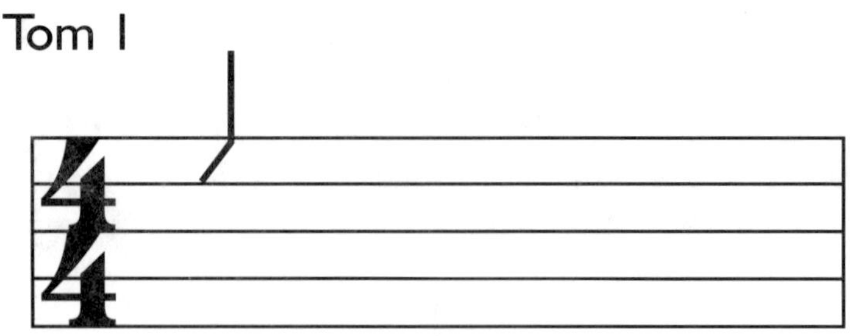

Tom #1 is written in the first space from the top.

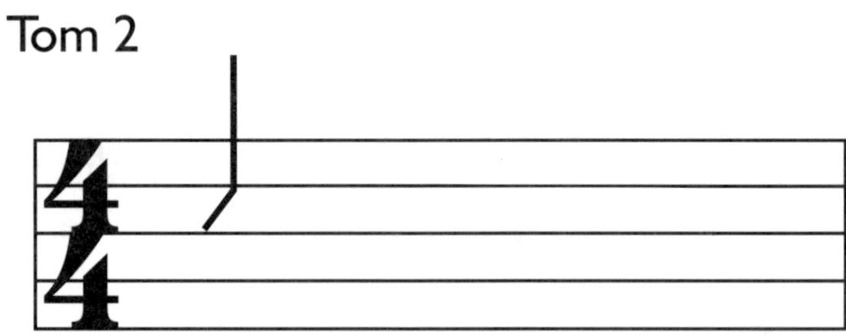

Tom #2 is written in the second space from the top.

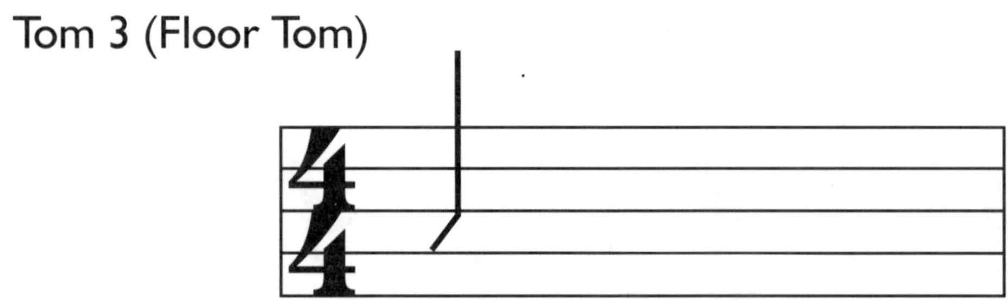

Tom #3 (floor tom) is written in the third space.

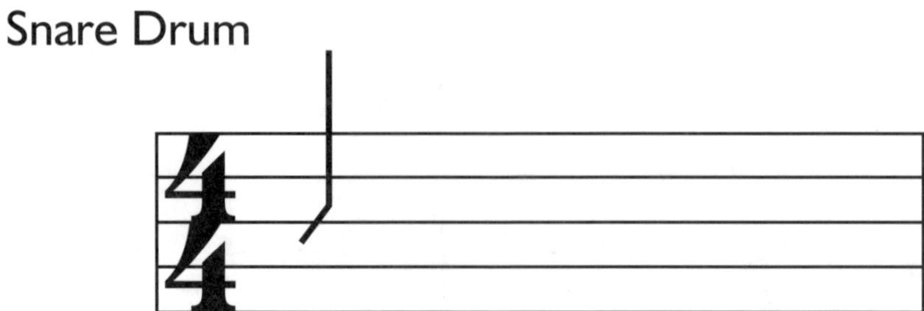

The snare drum is written on the middle line.

Bass Drum

The bass drum is written on the bottom line.

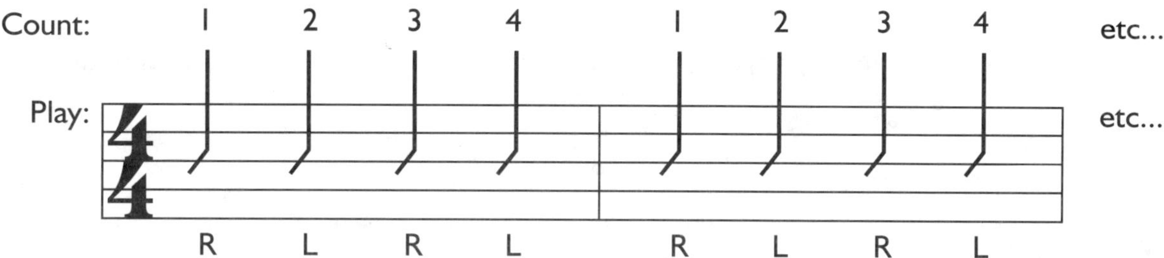

When you played alternating strokes, you counted and played quarter notes: 1,2,3,4.

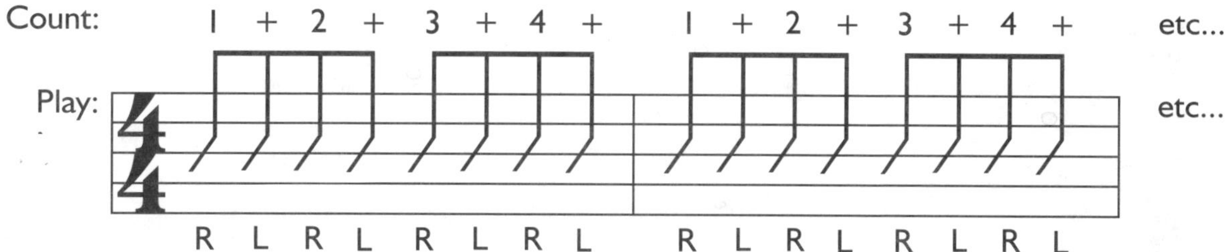

When you play twice as fast as quarter notes, you count and play 1 and 2 and 3 and 4 and. When you see the "+" sign you say "and". This is called playing eighth notes.

Eighth notes:

How To Apply Rhythms And Compose Drumbeats

Start by playing eighth notes on the hi-hat with your right hand.

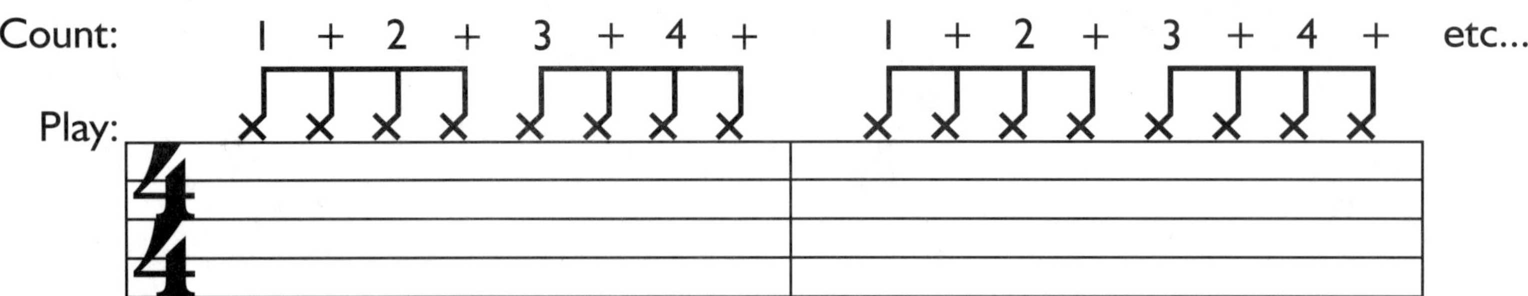

When you are comfortable with counting and playing the hi-hat part repeatedly, add the bass drum on counts 1 and 3.

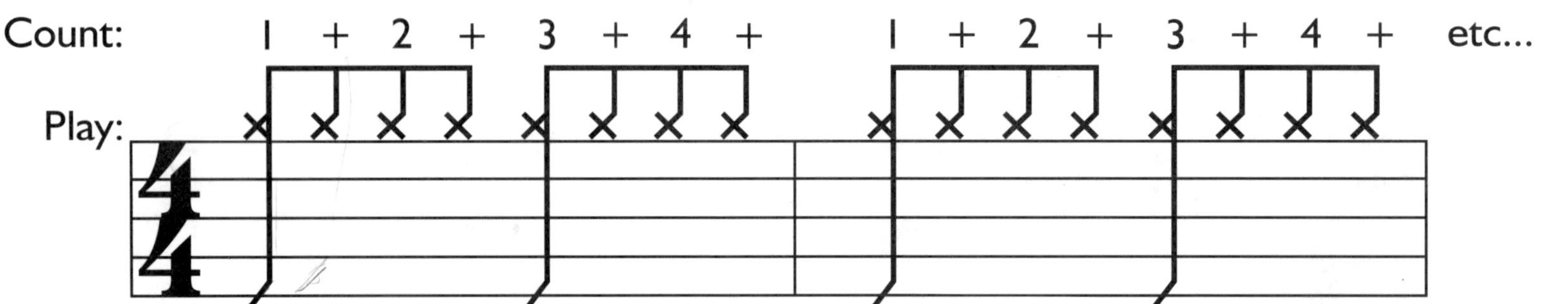

Tip: Notice how the bass drum and hi-hat parts line up on counts 1 and 3.

Now, add the snare drum on counts 2 and 4. We'll call this drumbeat #1. It is a one measure pattern that contains 4 counts.

Drumbeat #1

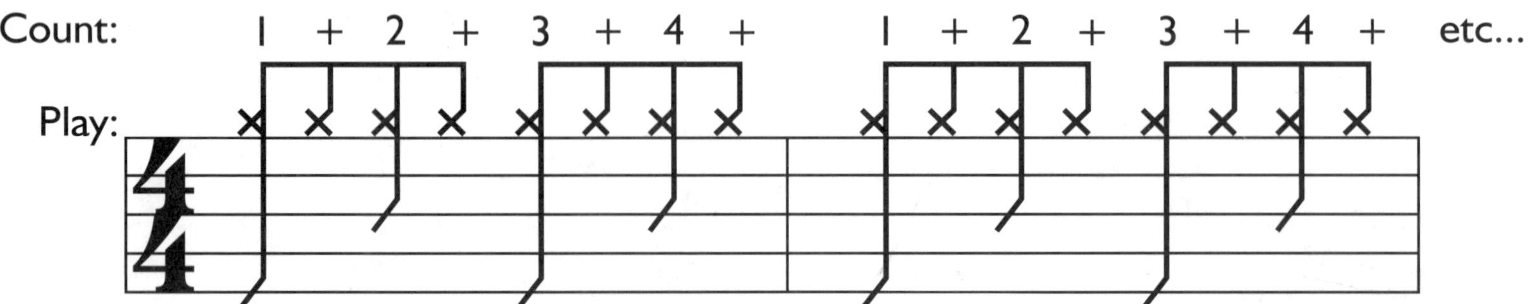

Tip: Drumbeat #1 is used on many popular songs. A good way to practice is to find songs with this beat and play along. You can also use this same basic pattern and vary it slightly to play other songs.

Drumbeat #2

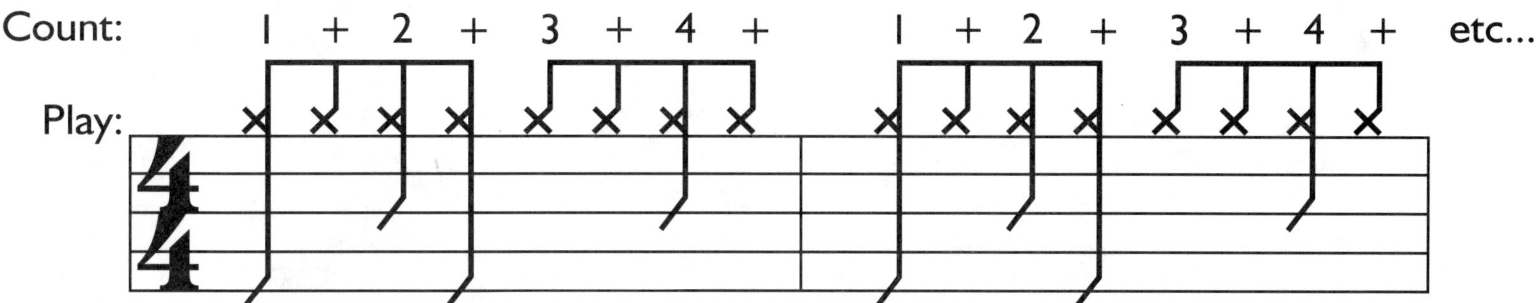

For drumbeat #2 notice that the hi-hat and snare drum part are exactly the same as drumbeat #1, except the bass drum part has been changed slightly. The bass drum is played on counts 1 and the "+" of 2.

Drumbeat #3

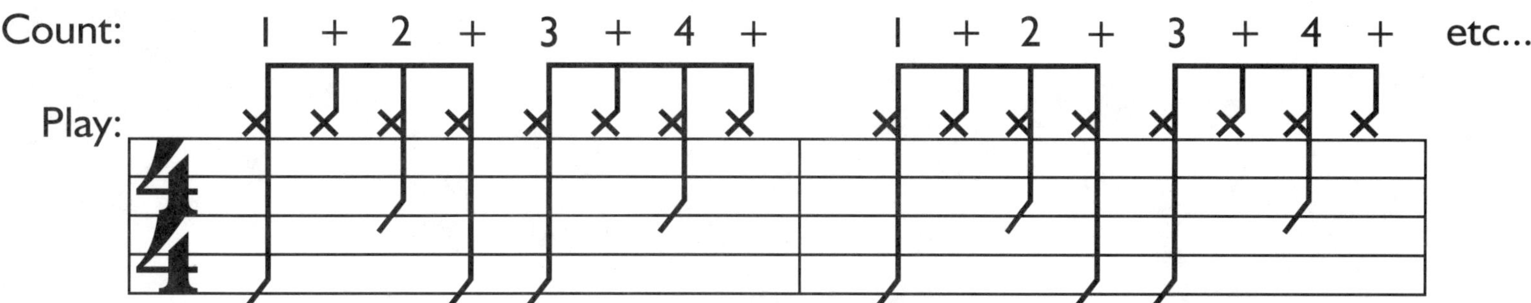

Drumbeat #3 is a combination of drumbeat #1 and #2. The hands play as above, except the bass drum is played on counts 1, the "+" of 2 and beat 3.

Tip: Before going on, spend some time practicing all three drumbeats.

DRUMBEAT VARIATIONS

Playing Cross Stick

You can add certain style variations to the drumbeats you just learned. The first style variation is called "playing cross stick". To do this, lay the stick across the snare drum head, with about 3 inches of the back of the stick hanging over the rim.

Next, place your left hand (palm down) over the stick on the drumhead and grip the stick between your index finger and your thumb.

While leaving the tip of the stick against the head, lift the stick and hit the rim.

Drumbeat #2 With Cross Stick

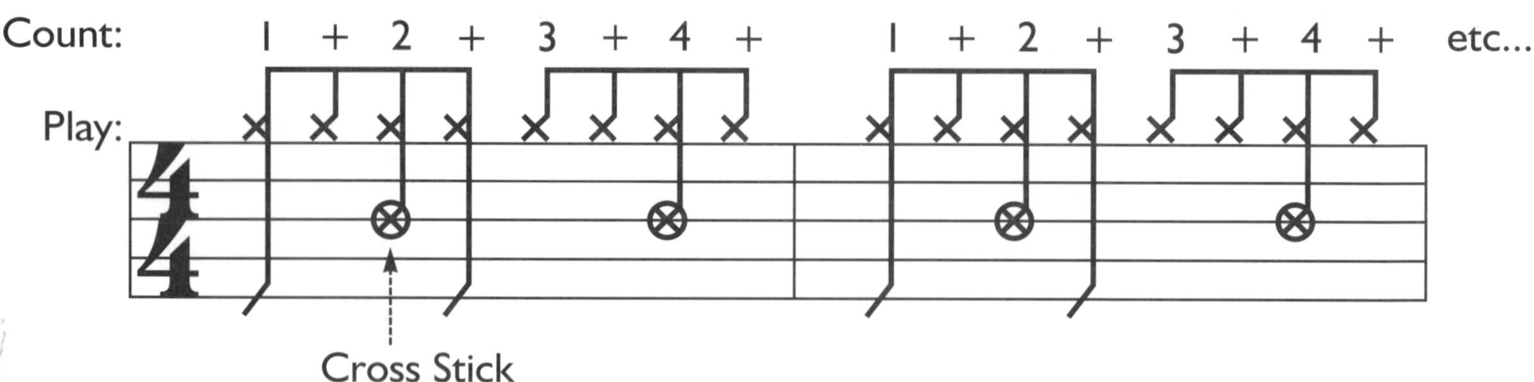

Play drumbeat #2 as you did before, except this time instead of hitting the drumhead on 2 and 4, play cross stick on 2 and 4.

**Note: This style is often used on ballads or during softer sections of songs.*

Drumbeat #3 With Straight 4 On The Snare

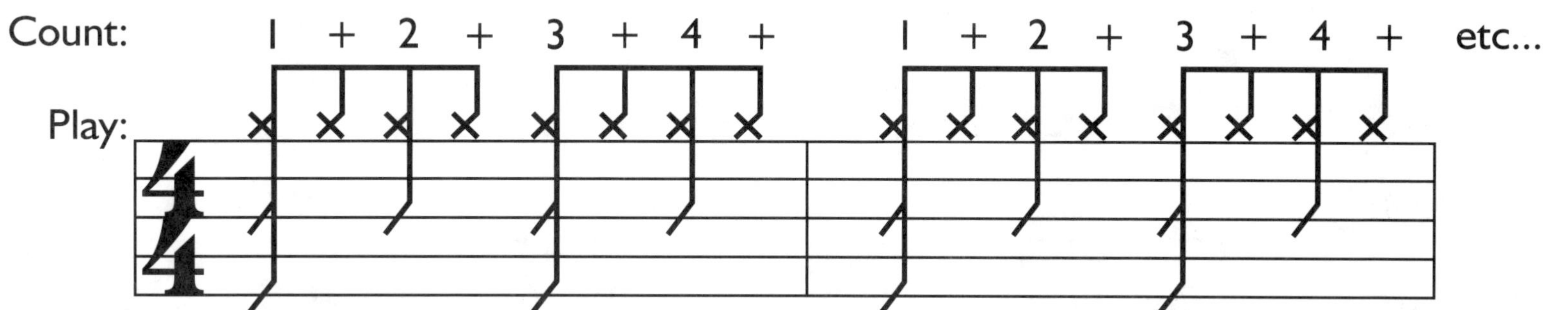

In this style variation, play all 4 beats on the snare drum while playing eighth notes on the hi-hat and 1 and 3 on the bass drum.

Tip: You can play any bass drum pattern you have learned with straight 4 on the snare drum.

Drumbeat #1 With Right Hand Moving To Different Sound Sources

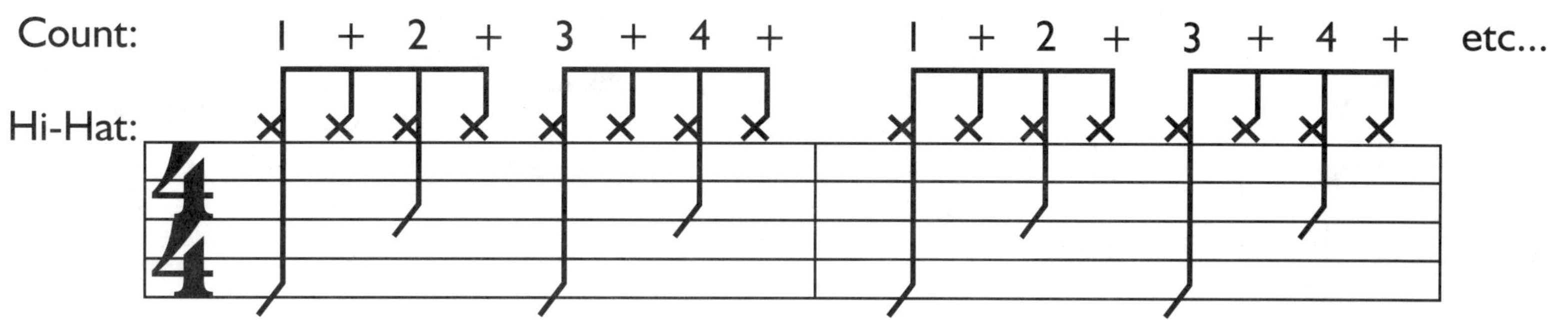

During the final variation, move the right hand to different sound sources. This is the easiest variation of all. Start out by playing drumbeat #1 with your right hand on the hi-hat.

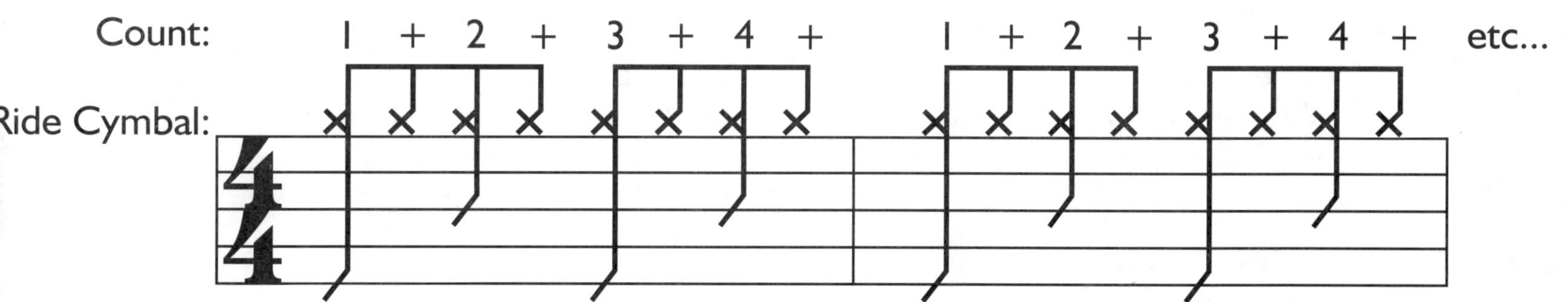

Without missing a beat, switch your right hand to the ride cymbal. Continue to play eighth notes. Notice that the pattern is the same, but moving to the ride cymbal gives the beat a new flavor.

DIFFERENT SOUND SOURCES

**Note: Try each sound source with the same beat.*

The Bell Of The Ride Cymbal

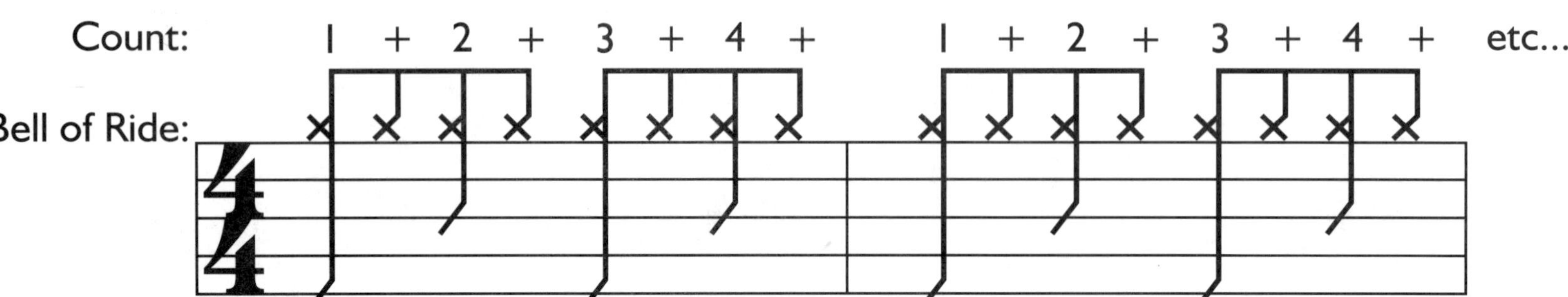

The Floor Tom

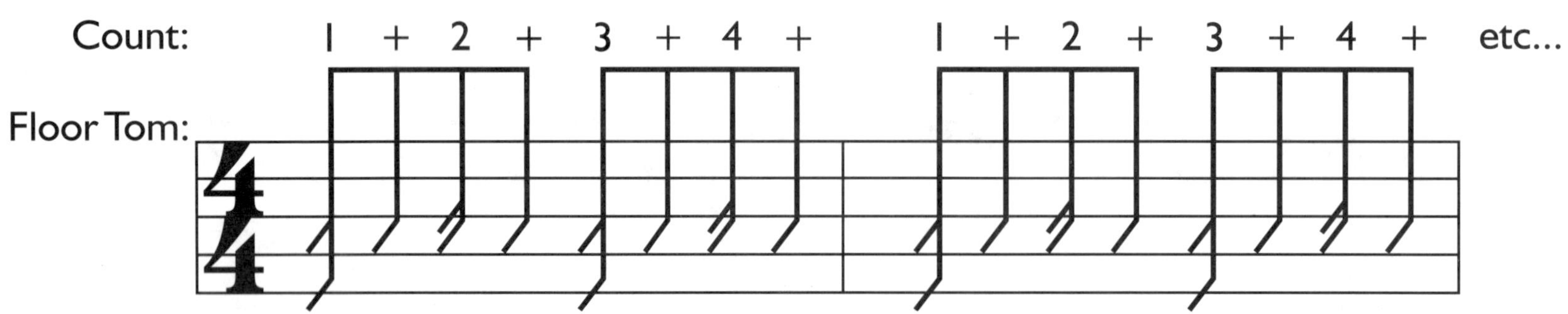

The Bell Of The Crash Cymbal

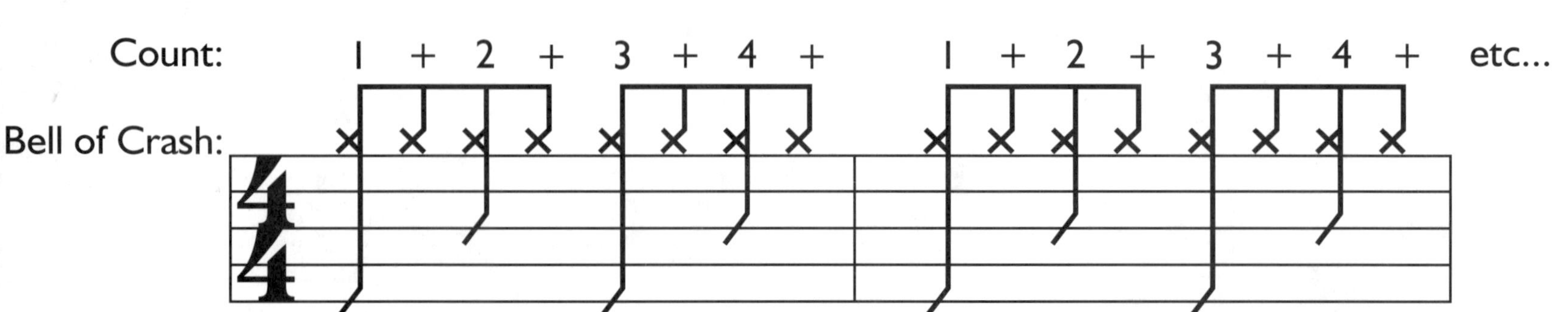

The beat stays the same, but different sounds are added on top. You can use these different sounds to help define the different sections of a song such as the verse, the bridge, and the chorus. Experiment by mixing the patterns and variations to compose your own drumbeats.

Use the blank staff pages at the end of the book to write down some of your own drumbeats.

CREATING DRUM FILLS

Songs are divided into different sections: the intro, the verse, the chorus, and the bridge. As the drummer, you can help connect these sections by using what's called a "drum fill".

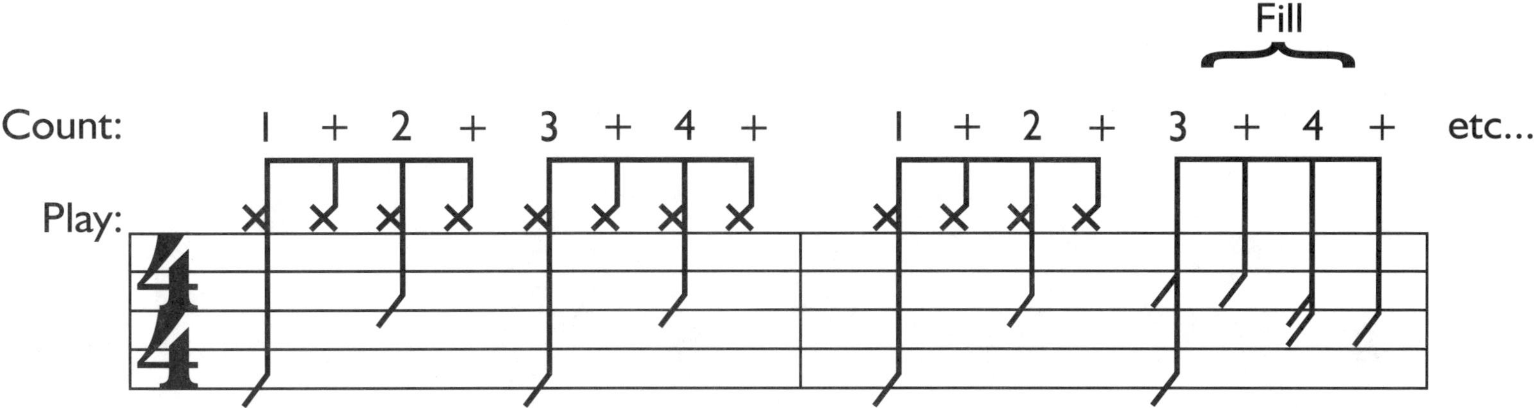

The second measure contains a drum fill.

The "fill" is the "break away" from the drumbeat. You are introducing something new.

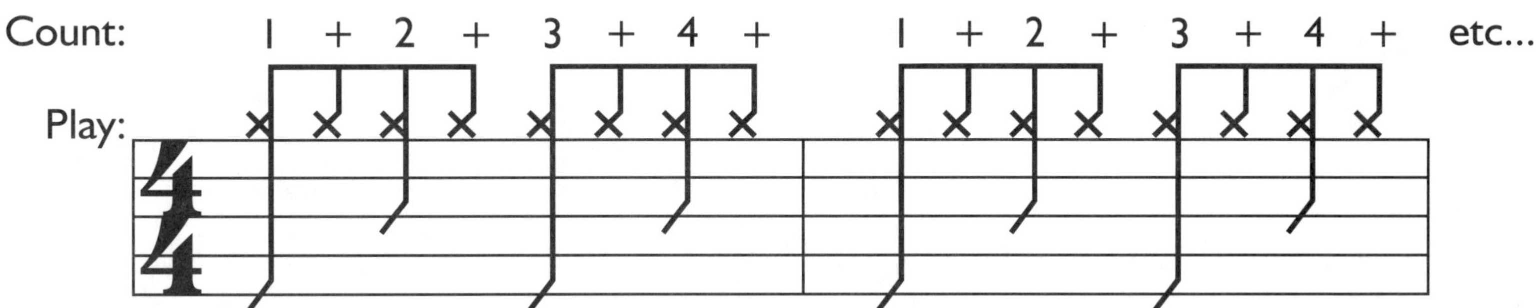

Play drumbeat #1, counting eighth notes.

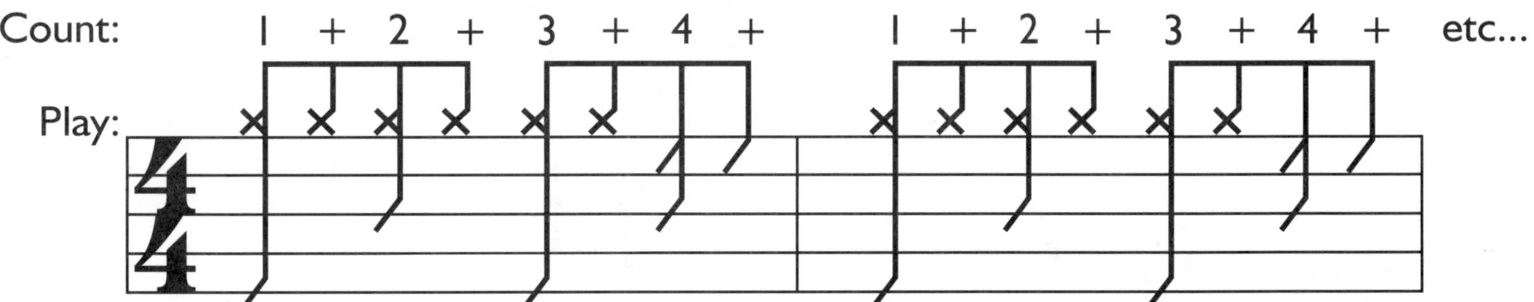

As you are "counting and playing", play tom #1 on counts 4 and the "+" of 4.

You are now playing a drum fill. Notice that you continue to play the same snare drum pattern on 2 and 4. Also notice that when you added the tom-tom, it was just an extension of the hi-hat part.

Now it's time for you to be creative. Just by moving your right hand to different sound sources, you can create many different fills.

The 1st tom and the bell of the crash cymbal

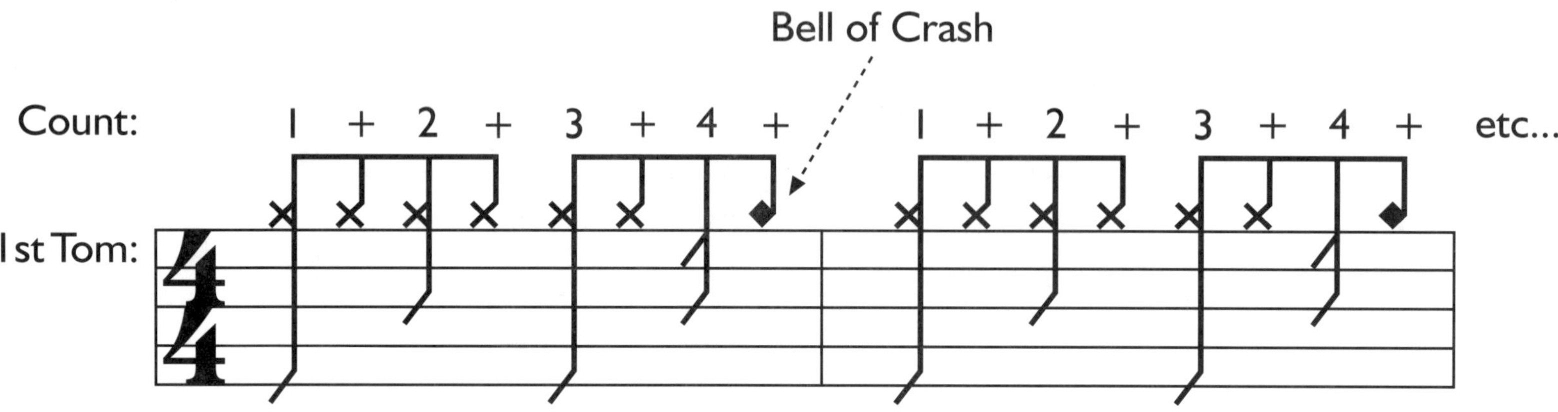

The 2nd tom and the bell of the ride cymbal

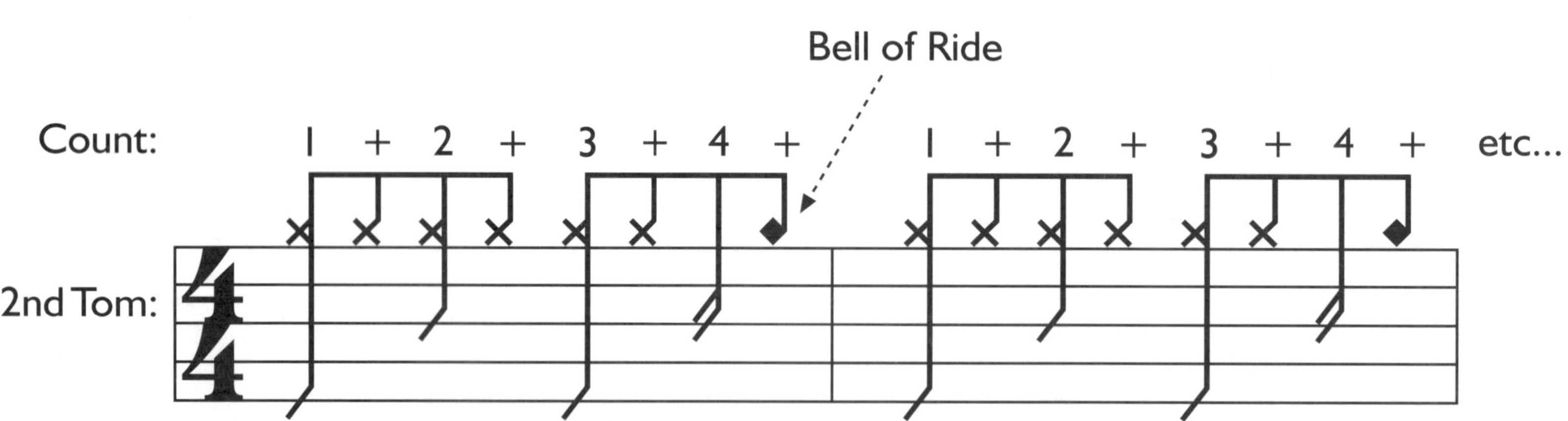

Start with these two examples and then make up some of your own.

Next, add a little more length to the fill. Playing the same drum beat and using the same counting, add one more note to the fill by starting on the "+" of 3.

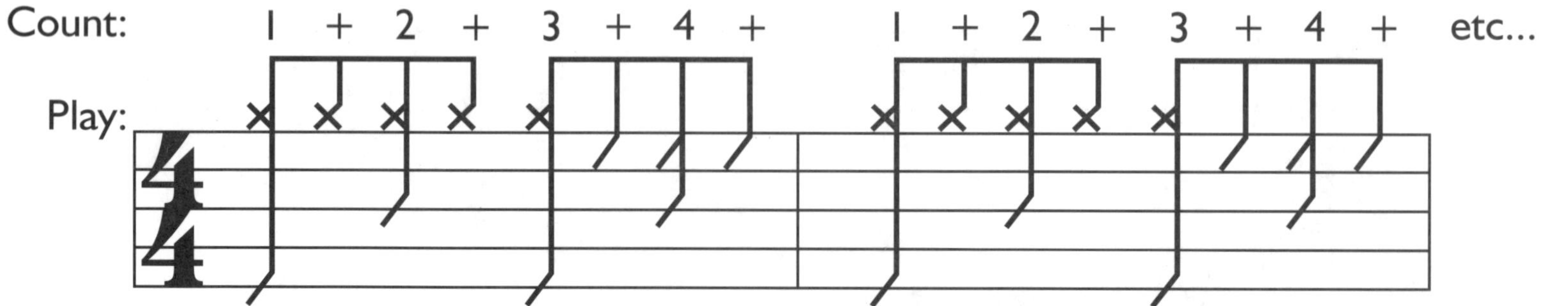

Continue to move around the set. Any three sounds in a row will work. Notice that you continue to play the same snare drum pattern on 2 and 4.

Start with these two examples; then make up some of your own.

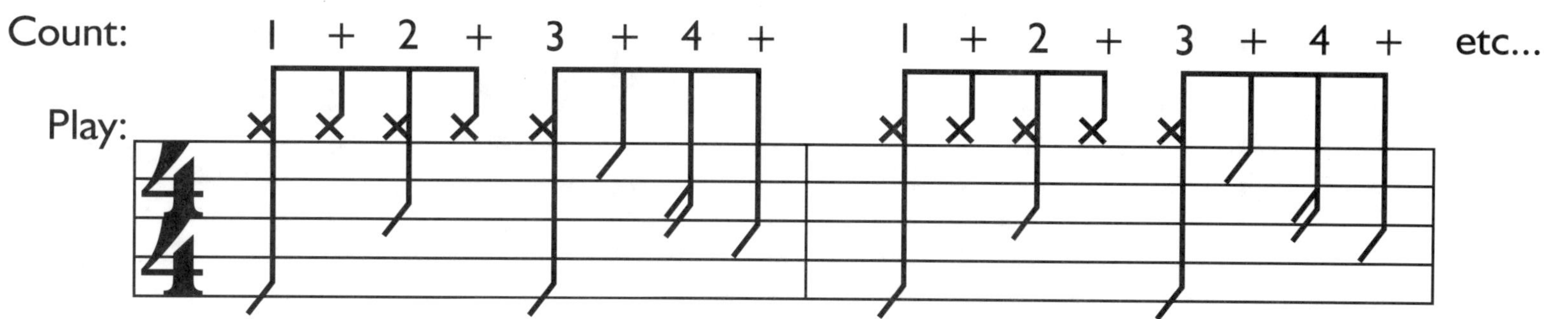

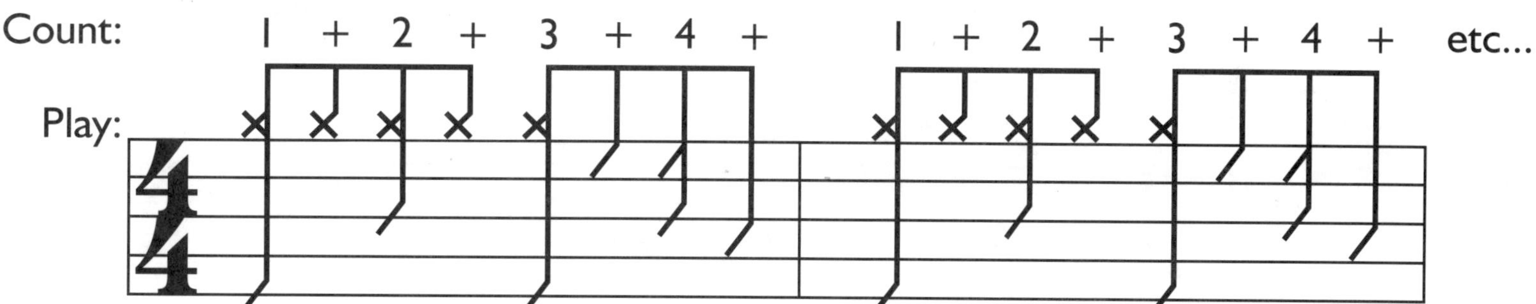

Tip: For variety, try using your brushes instead of drumsticks.

Now add one more note to the fill. Start the fill on beat 3.

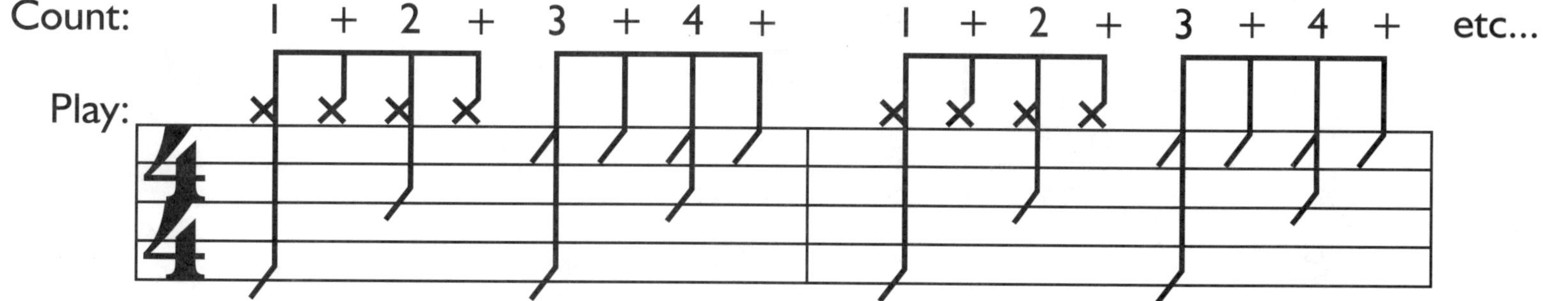

CREATING DRUM FILLS

Move around the set again. Start with these two examples; then make up some of your own fills.

**Note: Remember to think of the fill as an extension of the hi-hat part.*

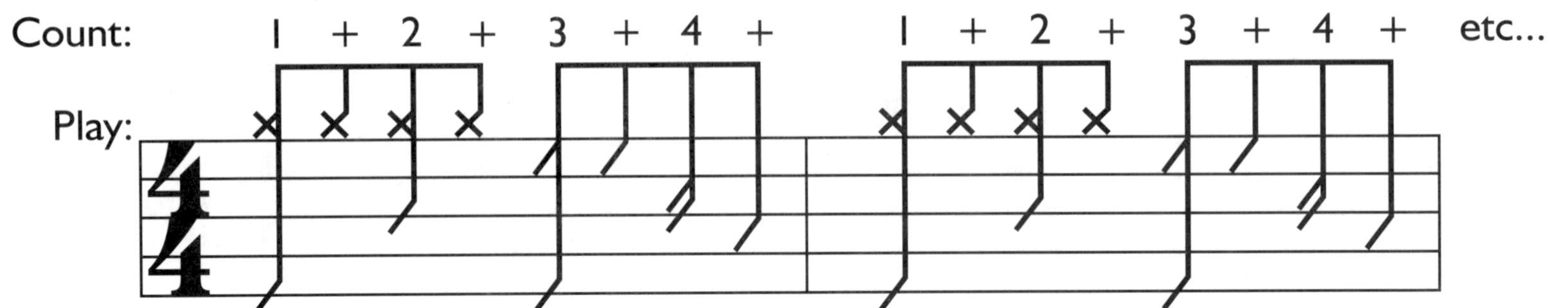

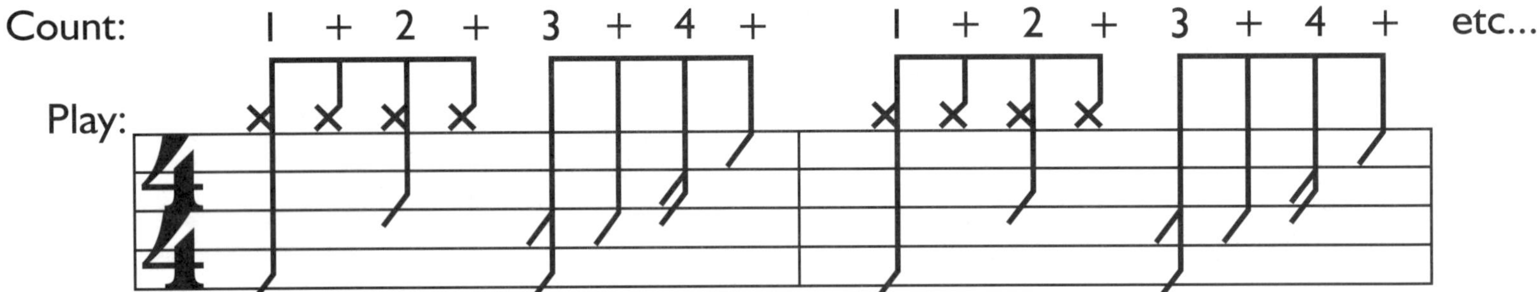

Here's how you can completely break away from the drumbeat and create a fill that is a little more interesting. In the first step, use both hands together for the fill. Start the fill on beat 3.

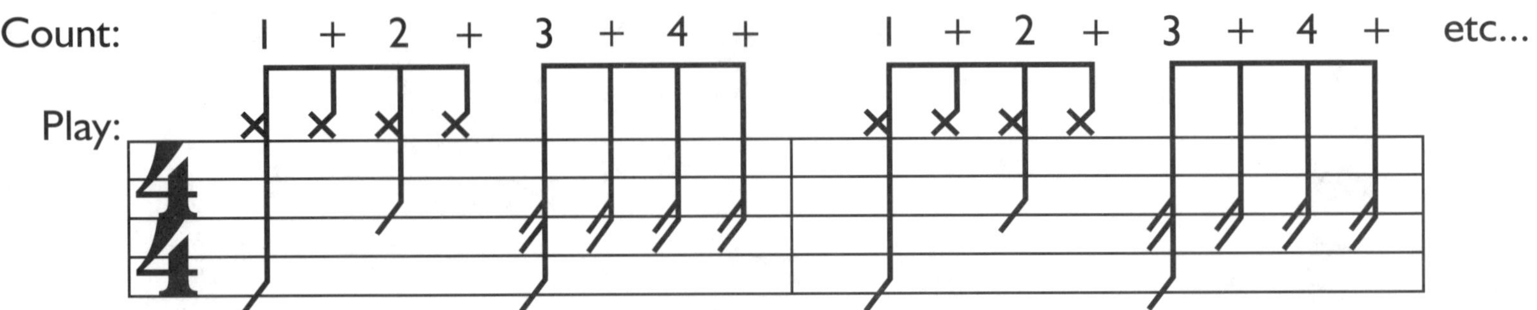

Another nice idea is to use the bass drum in the fill. Play the bass drum on beats 3 and 4 while playing the snare drum with your left hand and the floor tom with your right hand on the "+" of 3 and the "+" of 4. It is much easier than it sounds. Give it a try.

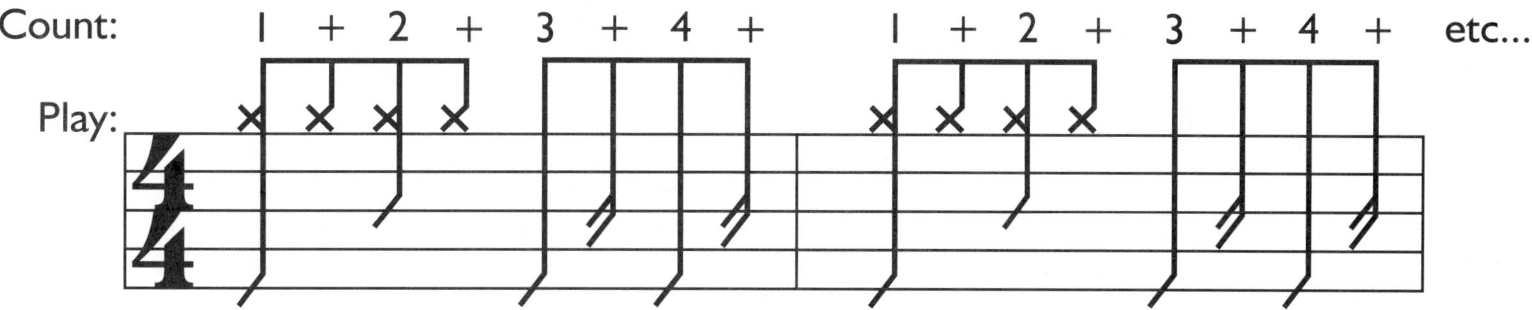

The final step to playing a drum fill is adding a cymbal crash. Notice the bass drum is played with the cymbal crash on beat 1.

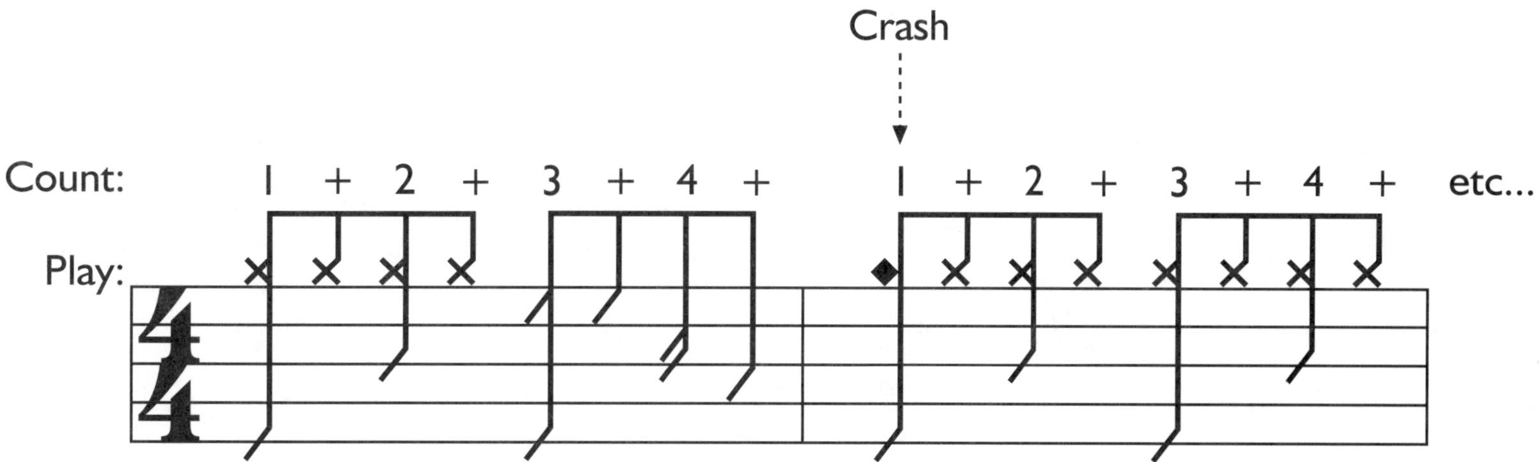

Be creative and make up your own fills. Try fills of different lengths and use all your sound sources. Remember to count and practice crashing with either hand.

Use the blank staff pages at the end of the book to write down some of your favorite drum fills.

EXERCISE SONGS (DRUM CHARTS)

The next section of the book is designed for your own personal practice and to use all of the beats, fills, skills, and techniques you've learned. A recorded version of these drum charts can be found in the video "Learn Drums on VCR" volume 1. The drum charts correspond to the exercise songs in the video songbook section at the end of the tape.

The drum chart for Exercise Song # 1 is in the style of "Stand by Me".

The drumbeat is written out for you in the first measure; after that you use "measure repeat" signs that look like this: "𝄎". A measure repeat sign simply means "play the previous measure again". You write out a new pattern only when something changes. This happens in measure 16 of the verse and in measures 1 and 8 of the chorus.

The eighth note counting (1+2+3+4+) is written to help you get started. As soon as possible you should become accustomed to counting only the number of the measure you are playing. The measure numbers are circled and are at the beginning of each measure.

As a drummer, you are responsible for keeping track of where you are in the song. You do this by counting measures. In the verse of Exercise Song #1, play drumbeat #2 (with cross stick) for 16 measures. Next, in the chorus, play drumbeat #2 for 8 measures. Connect all the sections with drum fills. The drum fills are played just before you switch to a new section (and before the end). The drum fills you've learned have been written out for you; however, feel free to play your own. Remember to crash on beat 1 after the fill and at the very end of the song.

At the beginning and end of the song, there are section repeat signs that look like this "𝄆 𝄇". They tell you to repeat a whole section of a song, or in this case, to repeat the whole song. Notice that when you start a new section, you start a new measure count as well. This helps you keep track of how many measures there are in each section. With one glance, you see that there are 16 measures in the verse and 8 measures in the chorus.

**Note: "fine" is a musical term that means "the end."*

The drum chart for Exercise Song # 2 is in the style of "Oh Pretty Woman".

This drum chart uses much of the same musical language as Exercise Song #1. It has measure repeat signs, measure numbers and different sections such as the intro, verse, chorus, and bridge.

For the intro, play drumbeat #3 (with straight 4 on the snare). During the verse, play drumbeat #3 for 10 measures. Next, repeat the intro for 4 measures, followed by another verse for 10 measures. Repeat the intro again for 4 measures; then play the bridge for 27 measures. You can divide the bridge into smaller sections by counting in groups of 8, 8, 4, and 7 bars. Repeat the intro for 10 more bars; then end with a cymbal crash on beat 1.

Don't let all the counting scare you; after you play through it a few times, you will get a feel for it. Just like in Exercise Song #1, connect all the sections with drum fills. The drum fills are played in the measures just before you switch to a new section. The fills you've already learned have been written out. Feel free to create and play your own fill ideas.

**Note: The symbol "〰" means to move on to the next measure without missing a beat.*

DRUM CHART FOR EXERCISE SONG #1

Count: 1 + 2 + 3 + 4 + etc...

VERSE

① ② ③ ④

⑤ ⑥ ⑦ ⑧

⑨ ⑩ ⑪ ⑫

⑬ ⑭ ⑮ ⑯ FILL

Crash

CHORUS

① ② ③ ④

⑤ ⑥ ⑦ ⑧ FILL

fine

32:42

DRUM CHART FOR EXERCISE SONG #2

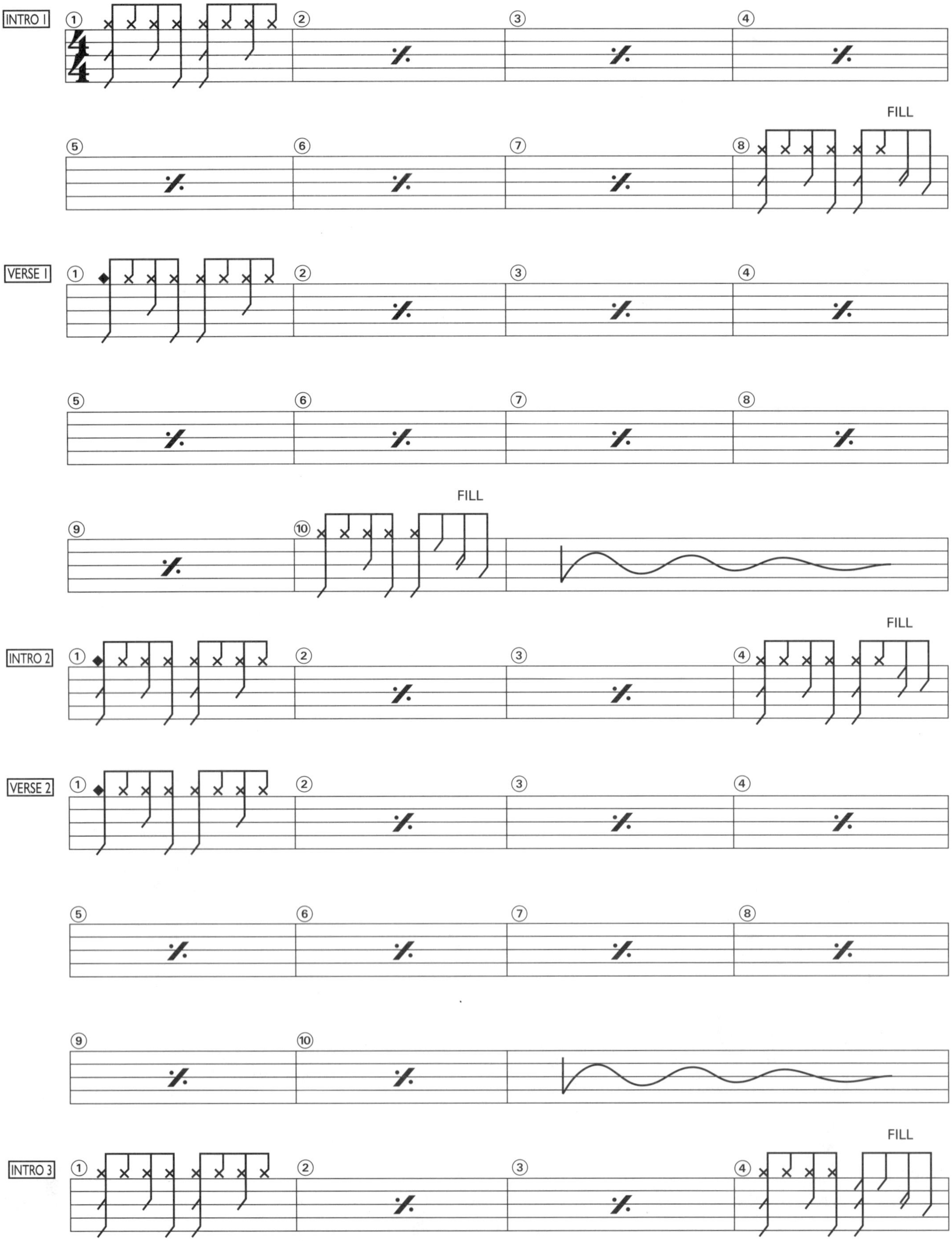

INTRO 1

① ② ③ ④

⑤ ⑥ ⑦ ⑧ FILL

VERSE 1

① ② ③ ④

⑤ ⑥ ⑦ ⑧

⑨ ⑩ FILL

INTRO 2

① ② ③ ④ FILL

VERSE 2

① ② ③ ④

⑤ ⑥ ⑦ ⑧

⑨ ⑩

INTRO 3

① ② ③ ④ FILL

Ride
1 + 2 + 3 + 4 + etc...
BRIDGE
① ② ③ ④
⑤ ⑥ ⑦ ⑧ FILL
⑨ ⑩ ⑪ ⑫
⑬ ⑭ ⑮ ⑯ FILL
⑰ ⑱ ⑲ ⑳ FILL
㉑ ㉒ ㉓ ㉔ FILL
㉕ ㉖ ㉗ FILL
INTRO 4
① ② ③ ④
⑤ ⑥ ⑦ ⑧
⑨ ⑩
fine

YOUR STROKE COMBINATIONS

The following spaces have been provided for you to write your own stroke combinations.

count: 1 2 3 4 1 2 3 4 1 2 3 4 1 2 3 4
play:

count: 1 2 3 4 1 2 3 4 1 2 3 4 1 2 3 4
play:

count: 1 2 3 4 1 2 3 4 1 2 3 4 1 2 3 4
play:

count: 1 2 3 4 1 2 3 4 1 2 3 4 1 2 3 4
play:

count: 1 2 3 4 1 2 3 4 1 2 3 4 1 2 3 4
play:

count: 1 2 3 4 1 2 3 4 1 2 3 4 1 2 3 4
play:

count: 1 2 3 4 1 2 3 4 1 2 3 4 1 2 3 4
play:

Blank staff diagrams have been provided for you to write your own beats and fills.

BLANK STAFF DIAGRAMS